In Paris CHAIRS are alive and well.

Chairs

Photographs and Text by
SHIRLEY C. BURDEN

An Aperture Book

HOW chairs came into being is a peculiar story.
Do chairs talk?
If they could what would they say?
I never thought about the answers to these questions
when I first started taking pictures of chairs in Paris

some years ago.
I found them in all sorts of peculiar places.
I thought they were beautiful
so I photographed them.
Some years later I ran across prints I had made of the chairs.
I still thought they were beautiful
but I thought I must have photographed them for other
reasons than beauty.
What kind of people sat on them each day?
Did they talk to each other about the people that used them?
Besides taking pictures I started to study
the people they served.

At first the chairs watched me in silence.
I guess they wanted to see how sincere I was.
Slowly I gained their confidence and they started to talk.
It's a peculiar feeling to have a chair talk to you
but most rewarding.
When I brought this manuscript to publishers they
were too polite to say I think you're crazy—some
even said I didn't know chairs talked.
My answer to that is
if you would only listen you would soon find out
bees talk to each other—birds talk—flowers talk
elephants talk—even whales talk.
There's a wonderful world out there
if you'll only listen.
A caring imagination is helpful too.

—SHIRLEY C. BURDEN

WHEN I first went to Paris
I was young.
I couldn't speak French.
I had no interest in photography
and I was lonely.
Later when I went back
things were different.
I was older.
I had found photography.
My eyes—my mind—my heart
for the first time
had become conscious of
the beauty around me.
I photographed
anything and everything.
I felt like a child
in a candy store.

MARQUESTE
1892

ONE day I was walking in the Bois,
one of the most beautiful parks
I think I have ever seen.

I MUST have been daydreaming
when I came upon this chair.
We all know chairs don't talk
but as I passed
I heard a voice say:
"I live in the parks.
I have no street address.
I have no possessions
but if you look
you can find me.
I'm always there."

AFTER that I kept a close watch
on the chairs I met in Paris.
I somehow felt they would love to talk to me
if I would listen.
Paris is well known for its beautiful women.
I ran across one in one of the parks.
She was young,
had a magnificent figure shaped like a heart
and slim beautifully shaped legs.
As I passed she looked up and said,
"You can't love alone."
If I had been younger
I would have suggested dinner
but even in Paris
you can't take a chair to dinner
without being noticed.

I MET a lot of chairs after that.
I became part of the family;
they knew I understood them.

I'VE gotten to know
this old girl very well.
She comes here every day
to sun herself
and dream of the past.

I WONDER if this child will ever learn I'm a chair, not a stepladder. What she sees in that man I'll never know.

IF only the lovers
would leave us alone.

THINGS are different these days, dear.
A wonderful night together wouldn't do either of us any harm.
What happens afterwards, well?!??!!

I TOLD her he was never coming back; but still she waits.

WE have to keep our eye on her. . .
her nurse is always gossiping with friends.

IT'S been a long day. . .
it's tough to be a goal post for a children's soccer game.

WHEN I went to the hospital
I told them my back hurt.
I never told them to remove it.

SHE'S here every day . . . I've tried talking to her
but she just sits there and stares into space.

I NEVER did understand the game.
When my husband tried to explain it to me
I understood even less.

WHY don't you let her sit on your lap?
You've seen boats before.

 I ALWAYS get the fat ones; I can't understand it.

FELLOW citizens. . .
If I'm elected
I promise—I promise—I promise.

DV

SHE'S always on the lookout for a man.
They say she's been married five times.

THEY say they came here for
peace and quiet,
but they fight more
over the card game
than they would if they were fighting
a war.

I LOST them in the war;
I wish I understood why.

NO George,
I don't know what they are doing,
but you are too old for such things anyway.

THEY pass me by
as if I weren't there.

I ALWAYS wanted to take a cruise but I never had enough money.

WE wish we knew
what to do with them:
they have very little money
and their children
have all left
and have their own families.

HIS wife died a month ago.
He writes a lot these days
to his daughter.

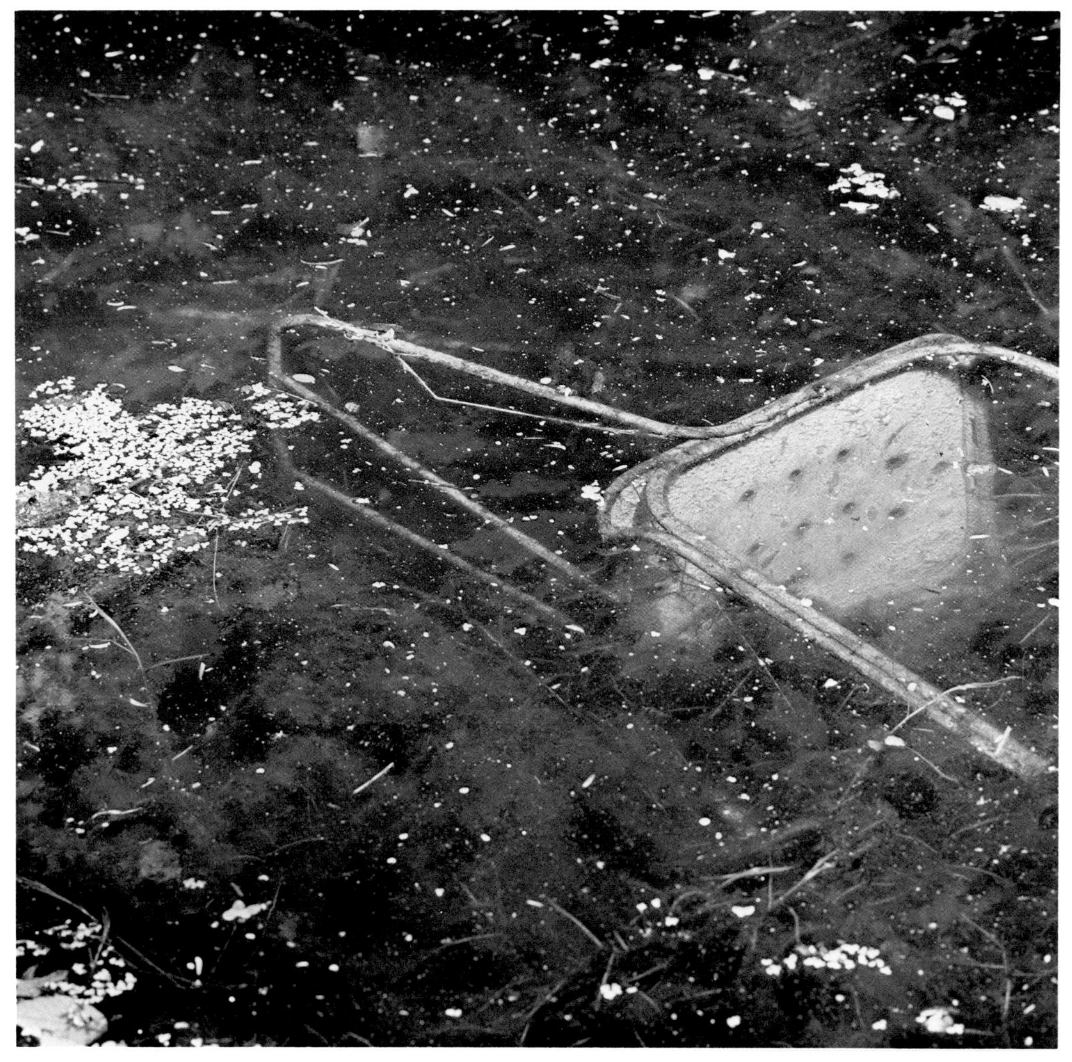

THERE are times it seems the answer
but it never is.

OUR friends have all gone
but we have each other . . . and we always have the pigeons.

SOONER or later
the sun sets on all of us. . .

GONE.
I hope not forgotten.

Distributed in the United States by Viking Penguin Inc.; in Canada by Penguin Books Canada Limited, Markham, Ontario; in the United Kingdom and Europe by Phaidon Press Limited, Oxford; in Italy by Idea Books, Milan; and in Australia by George Allen & Unwin Australia Pty. Ltd.
Aperture, a division of Silver Mountain Foundation, Inc., publishes a periodical, books, and portfolios of fine photography to communicate with serious photographers and creative people everywhere. A complete catalog is available upon request.
Address: Aperture, 20 East 23 Street, New York, New York 10010.
Other Aperture books are available from your bookseller or from Aperture.
ISBN: 0-89381-204-8; Library of Congress Catalog Number: 85-047825
Duotone negatives by Robert Hennessey, Connecticut. Printed by Stamperia Valdonega, Italy. Book design by Wendy Byrne.